OFF MY CASE

FOR KIDS

Other books in the Lee Strobel series for kids

The CASE FOR CHRIST FOR KIDS
The CASE FOR FAITH FOR KIDS
The CASE FOR A CREATOR FOR KIDS

Off My CASE
for Kids

12 stories to Help

YOU Defend

your Faith

Lee StroBel and RoBeRt ELMeR

zonder**kidz**

WILLOW
Willow Creek Association

ZONDERVAN.COM/
AUTHORTRACKER

The children's group of Zondervan

www.zonderkidz.com

Off My Case for Kids
Copyright © 2006 by Lee Strobel and Robert Elmer
Illustrations © 2006 by The Zondervan Corporation

Requests for information should be addressed to:
Grand Rapids, Michigan 49530

Library of Congress Cataloging-in-Publication Data

Strobel, Lee, 1952-
    Off my case for kids : 12 stories to help you defend your faith / by Lee
Strobel and Robert Elmer.
      p. cm.
    ISBN-13: 978-0-310-71199-5 (softcover)
    ISBN-10: 0-310-71199-1 (softcover)
     1. Apologetics—Juvenile literature. 2. Witness bearing
(Christianity) —Juvenile literature.   I. Elmer, Robert. II. Title.

BT1103.S78 2006
239—dc22

2006001095

Editor: Kristen Tuinstra
Cover Design: Sarah Jongsma and Holli Leegwater
Interior Art Direction: Sarah Jongsma and Kristen Tuinstra
Interior Design: Sarah Jongsma
Composition: Ruth Bandstra
Illustrations: Dan Brawner
Photography: Synergy Photographic

Printed in the United States of America

06 07 08 09 10 • 10 9 8 7 6

TABLE of CONTENTS

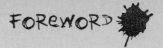

ReAd This First!

Sometimes there's a pretty wide gap between Sunday school lessons and real life, isn't there? On one hand, it's not hard to understand a Bible verse like 1 Peter 3:15: "Always be ready to give an answer to anyone who asks you about the hope you have." But...

Are you ready?

Well... maybe. But it's okay to admit that we sometimes let a chance to share our faith slip by. After all, for most of us, it's hard to think of just walking up to someone and telling them how much Jesus loves them—even if we know it's true!

So that's why you're reading this book: to help you see that everyday life is full of open doors to present the case for Christ, for our Creator, and for our faith.

You'll read twelve short stories of everyday kids in everyday situations. Well, mostly everyday situations. Maybe you've never worked for a family circus or ridden in a 3-G space simulator before. But no matter what, you'll be able to relate to the kids and the everyday jams they get themselves into.

Oh, and if any of the stories ring a bell in other ways, that's because they're built on ideas you might have learned in *The Case for Christ for Kids*, *The Case for Faith for Kids*, and *The Case for a Creator for Kids*.

In other words, these books explain many of the cool ways to help us better understand Bible truths. Things like, "Can we know Jesus was real by seeing what his disciples did?" Or, "How can we know there's a God by looking at the stars?" This book starts with those kinds of questions, but then shows us what might happen if kids draw pictures of the truth using their lives as pencils and paper.

Of course, they're not all perfect kids, and sometimes they mess up. But hey, what else is new?

You'll see how it works for Kaela as she runs down the hall at school—late for a concert she's supposed to play in. We'll stop by Shawn's Fourth of July picnic, where he tries to make a new friend feel welcome. Or sit down with Whitney in her science lab class the day she has to work with Josh, the juvenile delinquent.

If those don't sound like the ideal places to share our faith, read on. And most important, imagine yourself in each of the stories. That way, you'll start seeing how everyday stuff in your own life can open the door to faith in exciting new ways. Let the stories give you ideas of your own.

Now, if you haven't read the first three books yet, be sure to do that too. While the stories here include snippets of information from the other "Case" books, it's important to get the full story. It's a package deal.

More important, take a couple of minutes at the end of each story to answer the **Go Ahead, Stump Me!** questions. Don't worry! You won't be graded, and we didn't write them to give you a hard time. But we guarantee they'll help you start thinking about how to work these ideas into your own life. After all, that's what this book is all about.

So have fun with the stories, and as you read them you'll discover brand-new ways to make a case for Christ. We'll be praying for you. And see? It's not that hard after all!

Lee Strobel
Robert Elmer

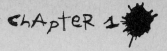

chapter 1

Lydia, Kid Missionary

Lydia saw it coming, but that didn't make it hurt any less. She stepped high over Mandy Witherspoon's outstretched foot so she wouldn't trip, but she lost her grip on her books. And the kids' giggles made her face flush like fire.

"Come on, let's go!" The bus driver looked up in the rear-view mirror and yelled at her. "And if you're late again to-morrow morning, you're going to have to walk."

Lydia held the tears in—just barely—scooped up her books, and scrambled off the bus as fast as her legs would take her.

"Speak English much?"

She didn't turn to see who had yelled the insult, but she could guess. Mandy Witherspoon. What did that girl have against her? She wished she didn't hear some of the taunts at school, wished she understood why some of the kids looked at her with so much hatred sometimes.

You don't belong here!

Get back over the border where you came from!

But we're not going back. Lydia stood in her muddy front yard for a minute, catching her breath and letting the rain wash the tears from her face. She didn't really miss what they'd left behind in Mexico. Except back there, everybody else was just as poor as Lydia and her grandmother. Just as poor, and just as desperate to find something better. At least here…

"At least here what, Lord?" she prayed out loud as she pushed open the front door to their apartment. Her thirteen-year-old sister wasn't home, as usual. And her grandmother would not return home for another two hours, maybe later, depending on what shift they gave her at the burger place. "What do we have now that's better than back home?"

Well, plenty, when she stopped to think about it. She sat down at the wobbly kitchen table and spread out her soggy books. Books, for one thing. A school to go to, and not all the kids were as mean as Mandy Witherspoon. A tiny apartment with a bathroom and a telephone. Three small rooms, which was not much compared to what a lot of other Americans had.

But compared to what they had back in Mexico? She would not soon forget the tar-paper shack they used to live in, her and a dozen other relatives: aunts and uncles and nieces and nephews, and all without a bathroom. She rested her head on her open English textbook for a minute, telling the Lord she was sorry for the way she complained. He had brought them here for a reason, she knew. She and Grandmother had prayed about it, looked for the answer.

"I'm sorry, God. Help me to know why I'm here, and what you want me to do."

But she was tired of trying to figure it out. Right now she would close her eyes for just a minute...

Lydia felt a soft hand on her shoulder, shaking her awake. Her grandmother stood over her, still in her fast-food uniform. Lydia didn't quite follow. She had just laid her head down a minute ago.

"What are you doing home so early?"

"How long have you been sleeping? It's almost six-thirty."

Lydia jumped up, nearly knocking over one of the grocery bags now on the table. She must have fallen asleep.

"And look at all this!" Her grandmother brought one last bag in from the hallway and set it down with a clunk on the kitchen table. She pointed to at least a dozen bags, now piled all over. Each one was stuffed with good things: canned peaches, a large ham, cranberries…

"I've never tasted these before." Lydia brought the can closer to see. Unreal. Everything looked so…

"And look here!" Her grandmother pulled out a large frozen bird. "Not just one turkey…two!"

Two turkeys! It was easy to dance about the kitchen, giggling at each new discovery, pulling out packages of marshmallows and spaghetti, canned tuna and sweet potatoes. So many strange foods. Did all Americans eat like this?

"A feast!" her grandmother cried, but then she stopped and looked Lydia in the eye. "But you didn't hear?"

"I didn't even hear you come in."

"Then who brought all this? It was all left outside."

Lydia had no clue, except that she'd heard church groups sometimes delivered groceries to needy families during the holidays. And they, it seemed, were one of those needy families. But when she looked at her grandma, they both smiled at the same time. For a moment they felt more like sisters than grandmother and granddaughter, *abuela* and *nieta*.

"Are you thinking what I'm thinking?" Lydia asked, and her grandmother nodded her head.

"I think so. We each take a bag, and come back for more."

"One bag for each house?"

That would be fine, so they pulled cans and hams from one bag to the other, spreading out the gifts they would take to others who were less fortunate than they.

God had given them this food for a reason, had he not? And this would be part of the answer to their prayers.

Lydia couldn't keep the grin from her face as they hurried out into the cold, driving rain. Now it didn't matter.

"Which house first?" she asked as they hurried down the street. That would not be the hard part. The hard part was getting away from the families who discovered them before they could get away. One older woman started crying and wanted them to come into her tiny apartment.

"Thank you, no." Lydia's *abuela* smiled and held her grand-daughter's hand. "We have more to deliver before it gets too late, and we're far from home. But…"

She paused, and Lydia filled in what they had already told a handful of other families. How much they loved Jesus, and how he had answered their prayers. Each time she said it to someone new, she felt a little less shy. He had given them so much, even before the groceries; otherwise, she knew, they would not be doing this.

And for the first time, Lydia knew it was really true. The old woman looked at them with tears in her eyes.

"But we just want you to know…," Lydia added, and it wasn't as hard to say now as it was the first time. "We want you to know how much Jesus loves you."

They left the old woman watching them through the window, and Lydia paused for a moment outside an older mobile home, looking something like the *Titanic* in its last moments. A dog growled from the darkness.

"Here?" Lydia wondered, still holding a grocery bag with their one remaining turkey. Her grandmother looked back at her with concern on her face. But Lydia didn't wait, just pushed open the gate and threaded her way past parts of a junk car as she walked up to the door. The dog went wild behind the door when she knocked.

"Anybody home?" She tried again, but no one came to the door. This would be one of the times they would just leave the bag of groceries on the front step and hope for the best. Oh, well. Lydia headed back down the walkway and almost reached the street when she heard a door squeak open. She turned around to find a girl standing in the light of the door-way, her blond hair framed in the light.

Lydia couldn't move. A streetlight flickered overhead, just bright enough to show the girl inside. So this was where Mandy Witherspoon lived.

"Merry Christmas." Lydia said, and it wasn't quite as hard as she thought. "And … Jesus loves you, Mandy."

How hard is it to share what you believe with people who will probably want to hear? What about with people you think may not want to hear? (Read Jonah chapter 4.)

_____

_____

Imagine you are in Lydia's position. Would you share *your* wealth? Why or why not?

_____

_____

How can you share more with others?

_____

_____

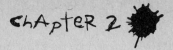

CHAPTER 2

The Greatest Show in Cincinnati

"Why can't you learn how to use a toilet like everyone else?"

Anthony scowled as he grabbed a snow shovel. Sure, he would clean up after her—but that didn't mean he had to like it. That didn't mean he had to like any of it, no matter how cool it might seem to someone on the outside. Nothing seemed cool when he had to clean up after a three-ton elephant every day.

Meanwhile, Penny rocked from side to side, the way elephants do, eyeing him suspiciously. Anthony's dad said that elephants could understand more than you knew.

Anthony wasn't so sure.

"Hey, kid, what's up?" An older man shuffled through the tent, his two-foot-long shoes flapping as he walked. Ricardo's eyes always looked kind of funny; he never seemed to be able to get all the clown makeup off his face.

"What's it look like?" Anthony kept shoveling. "Just the same old poop."

"Ah, so it's you against the elephant today, huh?" Ricardo stopped with his hands on his hips, like he was going to fix all of Anthony's problems. "You want to talk about it?"

Anthony just shook his head.

"Guess it wouldn't help to remind you how many other twelve-year-olds get to travel with the Bayley Brothers Family Circus, right?"

Give the clown credit. He was trying. Finally Anthony sighed and leaned against his shovel.

"I'm sorry." He wished he meant it. "Didn't mean to be rude. But you can't tell me any other kid my age would die for a chance to do what I do."

He chuckled as he looked at the wheelbarrow full of el-ephant dung. Most of what Anthony did was a lot of work. Work the ring during performances. Help the moving crews. Take care of the animals. Set up the sound system. Working in his family's traveling circus was just "everyday" life.

"Sometimes I just want to be normal," he went on, and his voice dropped to a whisper. "Not moving every couple of weeks to a new city. You know, have real friends, go to a real school?"

The clown bit his lip and rubbed some of the white makeup off his cheek with his shirtsleeve.

"You ever talk to your folks about how you feel?"

Anthony shook his head again and tossed the shovel aside. What good would talking do? The Bayley family had been running this circus for three generations, and everybody knew that Anthony would be the fourth.

Had anyone ever run away *from* the circus before? He hurried from the tent, out to the Cincinnati fairgrounds where they had set up, not really knowing which direction to turn.

He slowed when he neared a group of kids his age, the kind who liked to come to the show and make a lot of noise or eat a lot of junk food. Three guys and a couple of girls stood in front of a cotton–candy stand, and the guys were probably trying their best to look impressive. Two were twirling around on their bikes, doing tricks but not very well. Anthony pretended to stoop down and tie his shoes to hear what they were talking about.

"What's the big deal with the ropewalkers, anyway?" Biker number one almost fell. "I think it's all fake, like, the top of the rope is flat or something. Anybody could do it."

Anthony snorted at the dumb remark. He knew better; he'd tried it a time or two himself. And there was no trick, just hours and hours of practice with ropes and harnesses and stubborn performers who wouldn't give up. But when a couple of the girls looked over at him, he covered his mouth with his hand and coughed. One of the girls smiled at him.

Anthony strolled up a little closer to the group, looking for a way to hang out without looking too obvious. He fished out a couple of bucks from his pocket to buy some cotton candy, which gave him a chance to look like he was supposed to be there.

He hated cotton candy.

But he would stand by the group of kids while he ate it, listening while the boys trashed each circus act.

The clowns? Lame, said the guys.

The high wire? One of the performers fell into the net, which proved they were total amateurs.

The elephants? Dumb, and one of them couldn't do the sit-up-and-beg trick.

And the tiger tamer?

"I heard they drug the animals," said the second bike-twirler, and the other expert was nodding his head. "And did you see the trainer guy? He's got to be whacked to get in there with those things."

By the way they were grinning and nodding their heads, everyone seemed to agree.

"And besides that," he went on, "he looked like he wet his pants."

They all laughed at that commentary on the Bayley Brothers' most famous act, and Anthony felt his hands go cold when he realized he was smiling along.

Smiling along? Wait a minute. What was he doing?

"They don't drug the animals." He dropped the uneaten cotton candy into the trash and wiped his hands on his back pockets. "And the tiger tamer isn't whacked—or scared."

If they hadn't noticed him before, they did now.

"Well, excuuuze me." The guy who had been doing most of the talking made a face. "But who are you?"

"Anthony Bay—" He cut the last name short, and he was glad he wasn't wearing one of his bright orange Bayley Brothers Family Circus T-shirts. At least not this time. "Er, just Anthony."

"Okay, just Anthony. So they pay you to say that kind of thing?"

"I wish." Anthony shrugged.

Actually, he wished a lot of things. Wished he could say something smart. And that he'd found some other place to take a break from shoveling elephant dung.

"So what makes you the expert?" The kid on the bike number one wasn't going to let this drop so easily. What else could Anthony say?

"Because…my dad is the tiger tamer you're talking about." There. He said it. "And I guess I'd know if he was crazy or scared. In case you're wondering, he's not either."

Well, that pretty much did it. As the kids all stared at him, Anthony backed up a couple of steps and stumbled into the trash can.

"You're not kidding, are you?" asked the girl who had first smiled at him. "So is your dad really...Are you really...?"

"My last name is Bayley." Anthony dug a hand into his pocket and jerked his thumb at a hanging circus sign. "Yeah, that's me."

So much for making friends. Now he was back to being part of the freak show. Only this time, he wasn't so sure it was such a horrible thing. After all, he wasn't going to change his name or anything. And something in his pocket gave him an idea. He pulled out a fistful of free passes, the kind they gave out to newspaper reporters and other VIPs. He held them out to the group.

"Maybe you want to check out the show again, now that you know it's not fake?"

Well, who would say no to free passes? Anthony smiled as he gave them each one. This time, though, nobody mentioned lame clowns or drugged animals.

"So I'll see you at the show," he told them as he turned to go. And this time he looked up at the Bayley Brothers sign...

And smiled.

Go Ahead, Stump Me!

Imagine how Anthony felt when he heard people making fun of his father. What did he say that made a difference?

_____

_____

_____

Some people think Jesus hypnotized his followers and disciples. Others just make fun of him. What would you say to someone who acts this way?

_____

_____

_____

Read some places in the Bible that defend Jesus against people who would attack him. (Check out Matthew 10:22–33.) What does Jesus promise he will do for those who speak up for him?

_____

_____

_____

Think about how Anthony explained his father to the other kids. When you know someone well, like a parent or a friend, is it easier to explain the truth about them to others? Does that same idea apply when you talk about Jesus?

_____

_____

_____

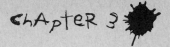

CHApTeR 3

PREDICTING STORMS

"And Josh, you're going to be working with Whitney on your weather-reporting project." Miss Peterson looked over the top of her glasses at the class. "Is that all right with you two?"

Josh shrugged and sort of grinned. "Cool."

No, no, no! Working with Josh Insley was definitely *not* cool, not even close. But what could Whitney do about it now, besides run from the room and never come back? This is what happened when she and the class druggie were both absent from Natural Sciences class at the same time.

Of course when Miss Peterson glanced her way, Whitney had no choice except to nod and smile like a cheerleader. *Thanks so much for ruining my life, Miss Peterson.* Smiling outside, screaming inside—but that was her life.

"All right, then." As far as Miss Peterson was concerned, the matter was settled with a quick clap of her hands. "We'll continue planning the projects in groups for the rest of the period. Josh and Whitney, you'll both have some work to make up, since you're a day behind."

Whitney covered her forehead and tried to think of a way to survive this nightmare. She could really only do one thing—do all the work herself, and allow him to cruise along with her for an A. This would be the only real option that would protect her perfect grade point average. And if Miss Peterson found out? Whitney would just tell the truth.

Josh just slumped in his chair with that glazed-over look of his. Ever since the eighth grade, he and his friends had always disappeared somewhere during lunch hour. She didn't want to know where. All she knew was that if she believed something, Josh was sure to make fun of it. He would argue against anything she said, anything she believed.

This was her science partner? She didn't wait, just started scribbling notes until Josh dragged his chair over to her desk.

"All right, partner," he drawled, "what's the plan?"

Whitney held her breath and tried not to breathe the ash-tray scent on his clothes. Could she get cancer from that kind of thing? She wasn't actually sure. But she knew they had to get going on this, especially since Miss Peterson was staring at them. Whitney scribbled her plans furiously, not looking up. "I'll read the report if you run the camera. You can do that, can't you?"

"You must really think I'm pretty stupid, huh?" He lowered his voice, and the back of Whitney's neck heated up. Finally she looked at him and bit her lip.

"No, I don't think you're stupid. Let's just figure out what to say about predicting hurricanes, and get this over with."

"Predicting hurricanes." He shrugged. "Fine."

At least he agreed with her on that. The thing was, he didn't turn out to be as dense as she had feared. In fact, as they dived into their research, she realized he knew the Internet much better than she did, probably because of all the raunchy sites she'd bet he visited. But Whitney didn't dare say anything about that.

"So you want to say something about this in the report?" he asked her as he drilled through some notes on how weather experts knew how to guess where hurricanes would go. The notes would become part of what Whitney was going to read on camera, as if she were a weather expert explaining the next hurricane. Like on TV.

"Sure, uh…" She did her best to keep up with what he was typing. At least they would be able to catch up to the rest of the class, no problem. But just because Josh was a little sharper than she'd expected, well, that didn't change his attitude. He looked up at her with a raised eyebrow.

"You going to try to slip in anything about how God makes the weather?"

Where had that come from? She snapped her mouth shut, trying to figure out how to defend herself.

"I don't know," she finally admitted. "Although maybe it's not such a bad thought."

He put up his hands. "I wasn't trying to give you ideas."

"You brought it up, not me."

Half an hour later he would bring it up again. Only this time they were out in back of the auditorium, where Josh had the school video camera trained on her, and she was getting ready to read their script about predicting hurricanes. Kind of reminded her of the youth group video scavenger hunt they were planning at church, only this time she had to hold on to her hair to keep from being blown away. And this time she was rethinking their idea to do this outside.

"So if your God knows all about the weather," Josh asked her as he looked up at a dark cloud, "how come he doesn't give us a better clue, sometimes?"

She noticed the camera's red light blinking at her. The tape was rolling? Was he trying to make her look foolish?

"We just have to know where to look, I guess."

"Yeah, right. Sounds pretty convenient." He adjusted the camera on its stand as she spoke. "You pray, and God tells you the future, a hundred percent. Just like he tells you the winning lottery ticket numbers."

"Maybe not the lottery ticket numbers." Whitney knew where she was taking this now. After all, she might never have a chance to talk to this boy again—or want to—on camera or off. "But sometimes he does tell the future."

"No kidding? Now THAT I would like to see."

"Then all you have to do is check out the Old Testament."

"I KNEW it! You mean like the secret Bible code."

"No, no. Nothing bogus like that. Just dozens of predictions about how Jesus would come. Actually, I don't know how many, but there were a whole lot."

"Like about what?"

"Like what he would do. Even how he would die."

"I heard there was a guy named Nostradamus who did some of that kind of thing. Told the future."

"No, no. NOT like Nostradamus. This was all written in the Old Testament, hundreds of years before it happened. And every prediction was one hundred percent on. So it wasn't like a fortune-teller…or a hurricane prediction."

"Hmm. A hundred percent?" Josh scratched the peach-fuzz goatee on his chin, like he didn't believe a word she was saying. At least this time he didn't have a snappy comeback, so maybe he was thinking about it.

And still the camera blinked, so she figured she'd better pick up her script and start talking about how to predict hurricanes. But that's when a gust of wind lifted up a trash bucket and sent it scuttling their way.

"Whitney!" Josh yelled at her. "Watch it!"

This was no hurricane, but—

"Keep the camera rolling," she ordered, just as the sky opened up and dumped a thunderstorm full of rain on their heads, just as the trash bucket bumped by behind her. Josh got the idea and grinned as she recited the introduction to their report.

"Is the next hurricane going to be a level one, a level two, or even stronger?" She cupped a hand over her face to shield the rain, now pouring and matting down her hair. "It's hard to tell, and scientists don't always know…"

A gust of wind nearly ripped the script from her hand, but she kept going. "Unless they know how to look for the right clues."

Go AheAD, StUmP Me!

How do you think all those prophets knew that Jesus was coming? Do you think it was coincidence?

_____

_____

What would you say to someone who might think all the prophecies were written AFTER Jesus was born?

_____

_____

_____

How do you treat someone who dresses or acts differently from you? Are you afraid to talk to them? If not, how do you feel?

_____

_____

_____

chapter 4

DiD You See ELViS?

"Lord, we want to be good examples for you, but..." Nate kept his head bowed as he and Aaron prayed in the back room behind the stage. No one would see the two friends there, for now. The only thing was, Nate couldn't keep his hands—or his voice—from shaking.

"But when everybody in the audience is going to be staring at us," Aaron said, picking up the prayer, "it's pretty tough."

No kidding. Nate wasn't sure he liked being reminded, but it was true. Every mom, dad, and grandparent was sitting out in the Franklin Middle School auditorium, waiting for the annual talent show to start. Plus their youth pastor, Bill Stewart, and a bunch of people from church. Not to mention a photographer from the Franklin *News-Dispatch*, who was probably there to take a picture of the $250 first-prize winner.

Was it too late to slip out of the building, maybe hide in Aaron's basement?

"So please help us not to croak in front of everyone." Nate finished up the tag-team prayer. "In Jesus' name—"

Almost. The storage-room door burst open before he got to the "amen," and a guy with long, painted-on black sideburns and a glittery white suit poked his head inside.

"Whoa!" Elvis stepped back for a moment, then grinned like a fisherman with a big fish on the line. "A-MEN, brothers! I be-LEEVE!"

Too bad you don't really, thought Nate. Not that they hadn't tried, like inviting him to youth group for the past umpteen years. At first they'd thought he might be interested, since his grandpa had been some kind of famous preacher. But all they'd ever heard back were the usual dumb lines, like "Yeah, I'll come, maybe next year."

Well, next year came and went, and Jeremy was a tough case, all right. Smart—and he knew all the Christian lingo. The weird part was, he could curse like a sailor one minute and tell a crazy joke the next. And now he blocked the door, wearing that teasing grin of his that sent a chill up Nate's spine.

"Except praying isn't going to help you much," he told them. "Not when you're up against the King."

"Ha!" Aaron blurted out. "All you're doing is imitating some singer guy who died years ago. What's so cool about that?"

"Aaron." Nate elbowed his best friend. Aaron was pretty good at saying whatever came to his mind, usually before he thought it through. But it was too late. Jeremy had already taken the challenge, and his dark eyes narrowed when he looked at them.

"And all you're doing is praying to some religious dude who got himself killed two thousand years ago, and all his buddies besides. Tell me, what's the difference?"

Whoa. Nate shivered like they'd just been hit by a blast from a quick-freezer. And no, they hadn't seen this side of Jeremy before. Not quite. Aaron choked on his spit.

"Hey, relax, man." The easy grin crept back on Jeremy's face. "If it works for you, no problem. Make you feel better? I just came to say that I hope you weren't planning on winning the show, 'cause—"

"We'll make you a deal," Aaron interrupted. "If we finish ahead of you, all you have to do is come to our youth group party afterward."

Dude. Nate was ready to slide off his chair, because his best friend had a death wish. But Jeremy only seemed to think a moment before he grinned and held out his hand.

"Deal. And if I finish ahead of you…" He paused. "You promise to stop laying all the Jesus stuff on me. Forever. I already heard it all from my grandpa."

Aaron looked him straight in the eye and shook the other boy's hand. Only with the costume and all it looked like he was shaking Elvis' hand, which was kind of comical, so Nate did his best not to think of it that way. Jeremy scowled at him.

"Something funny?"

"No, no." Nate zipped his lip and shook his head. "We probably need to get ready, though."

"Ten minutes, Brother Nathan." The Elvis impersonator straightened his swoopy-haired black wig. "Break a leg."

Weird. Nate wasn't sure what made him shake more—their strange bargain with Jeremy Winston, or the talent show itself.

"We'll be there." Aaron made for the door.

"I'll tell Mrs. Mac you're going to open the show in prayer," Jeremy joked.

Knowing Jeremy Winston, he just might.

"How about if I pull his microphone plug in the middle of his act?" Nate mumbled as he clenched his fist and followed Jeremy to where everyone was gathering behind the stage.

"Oh ye of little faith." Aaron looked all business. "We're going to win. And we still have to be a witness."

"A witness, yes," Nate whispered back. "Not a joke."

Nobody said their two-man juggling act was going to be serious. At least their show was pretty good, since they had been practicing for the past couple of months in Nate's garage. So when it was their turn they dropped the bowling pins only once, and people clapped at the end of the act.

"Pretty good, huh?" Nate said it only loud enough for Aaron to hear, and they bowed once more before they left the stage. Everybody slapped them on the back or gave them a high five. Even Jeremy.

"Not bad." Jeremy adjusted his costume once more. He was up next. "Maybe you'll get second or third."

Well, it didn't take long to figure out they weren't placing first. Nate had to admit it: Jeremy was good. Awfully good. When it was his turn, he did the Elvis shimmy, the Elvis slouch, the Elvis voice. He even grabbed the microphone and

twisted it around like Elvis. A bunch of girls in the front row screamed for fun. And after Jeremy finished telling everybody they weren't nothing but a hound dog, the audience even gave him a standing ovation.

"Thank you." Jeremy smiled out at the crowd in excellent Elvis form. "Thank you very much."

Nate even caught himself smiling and clapping with the rest of them. Whoops.

Aaron punched him in the arm. "Whose side are you on?"

"Sorry." Nate shrugged. "He was good."

The problem was, Jeremy knew it too.

"No hard feelings, huh?" Jeremy met them as he strutted off the stage. "The King was just… too good for the Bible Boys, I guess."

Nate could imagine the steam pouring out of Aaron's ears. But he forced himself to shake Jeremy's hand.

"You did a good job playing a dead guy," Nate told him.

"Don't you read those newspapers they sell in the supermarket checkout lines?" Jeremy laughed. "People have seen Elvis alive, like in a Seven-Eleven in Arizona."

"Okay." Nate played along. "But what if Mrs. Mac said she'd flunk you unless you admitted the truth—that Elvis was dead?"

Jeremy stopped rubbing at the stage makeup on his face long enough to give them a curious look. He'd won his bet, but there really weren't any other ways to answer the question.

"Seriously." Nate pressed his point, since they might not get another chance. "What would you say then?"

"If I was going to flunk? What do you think? It's just a joke, okay? Nobody's going to take a hit for something they don't really believe."

"Bingo." Nate snapped his fingers. "So don't you think all the disciples were telling the truth about Jesus—especially when they were willing to get killed for it?"

The Bible Boys left Jeremy standing backstage in his Elvis costume, holding his wig and looking more confused than they'd ever seen him.

"You're still welcome to come to youth group," Aaron added with a smile. "Except, whoops! Sorry. We're not supposed to mention it to you anymore."

Somehow Nate figured it didn't matter, this time. And he had a feeling Jeremy might finally show up.

GO AheAD,
StUmp Me!

Imagine you were a friend of Lazarus when he died. You're sad — but then he walks back into the room! What do you think about that? (Read the story in John 11.)

_____
_____
_____

What would you say if someone asked you, "Come on, now. A dead man can't really come back, can he?"

_____
_____
_____

Do you think Jesus was really dead in the first place? And if you do, why do you think Jesus came back?

_____
_____
_____

Imagine you were one of the first disciples. Would you have died for something you didn't believe in — or that you knew wasn't true? What does history tell you about what the disciples believed?

_____
_____
_____

35

CHAPTER 5

SCAVENGER HUNT

"So here's the drill, Jess," announced Matt as Jessica climbed in back next to Alyssa. He'd just picked her up in his crazy little yellow and orange and blue Volkswagen Beetle; Sarah rode in the front passenger seat.

"We're up against three other teams, and we're each going out with a video camera rolling."

So far, so good, thought Jessica. *This wasn't going to be too hard.*

"We're supposed to record people answering our Bible trivia questions," he added, "only we can't tell them the answers before they meet us. Everything's live on camera. It's supposed to be fun, and maybe even funny. I mean, people might say some funny things."

Okay…

"And the first team that gets back to the youth group room at church with all twenty-five of the right answers caught on tape wins."

Unsure, Sarah said, "I'm just thinking it had better be good." She was probably afraid the rain was going to mess up her hair.

Jessica looked over at Alyssa, who always had a big-eyed expression, like she was a deer caught in the headlights. She carried a Bible everywhere she went and wore a big cross around her neck.

None of that was *bad*, of course. It was just that Sarah and Jessica were exactly like all the Christians Jessica had ever known when she was growing up in Detroit. And she hadn't expected to find them in San Diego.

On the other hand, Matt was very cool—in fact, he was one of the main reasons Jessica became a Christian the month before and got baptized in front of everybody. He was telling jokes and driving them to the next place on the map, having fun the whole way. He was a great guy to look up to—kinda like a big brother.

"So there's this Sunday school teacher," he said, "and she's trying to tell a story to her fourth-grade class, right?"

Right. This is a joke? Jessica wondered.

"And so the teacher asks her little kids what's little and gray, climbs trees, eats nuts, and has a big, bushy tail."

Jessica was definitely not sure where Matt was going with this.

"And the little kid says, 'I know the answer's supposed to be Jesus, but it really sounds like a squirrel to me.'"

And they all laughed, except Jessica.

Maybe that's because they were all raised in Sunday school, she thought, *and I wasn't.* "I don't get it," Jessica said carefully.

"Don't worry about it." When Matt smiled, he had a way of making people relax. And by that time they were pulling up to the next house anyway, so they didn't have a chance to explain the joke to her.

But one thing Jess was pretty good at was asking questions. So naturally they put her in charge of the clipboard. Matt was working the camera, while the two other girls reviewed directions to the next houses. Sarah was still messing with her hair.

"Whose house is this?" Alyssa wanted to know, and Jessica told her it belonged to an older couple named Al and Betty Wilson. Sounded like old people names to Jessica. But they were nice, and they were smiling when they opened the door. Pastor Jason had prepped them, so they knew the team was coming.

After the Wilsons seated themselves on the couch and the camera started rolling, Jessica asked, "And our question this time is… what was Abraham's hometown?"

They hardly blinked, like someone had asked them who the president of the United States was.

"That would be Ur."

Mrs. Wilson smiled and squeezed her husband's hand, and he added: "Ur of the Chaldees."

Ten down, fifteen to go. They thanked the Wilsons, checked them off the list, and piled back into the Beetle.

"Hey," said Sarah, pulling down the little mirror to see if her makeup was smudged. "Maybe we're going to win the pizza party."

No one would have said that was a bad thing. Jessica wondered aloud how all those people knew the answers to so many off-the-wall Bible questions. But Alyssa just shrugged and looked at Sarah. They were raised in a Sunday school room too. And kids like that were usually the ones who said the answer was "Jesus," when the answer was really "squirrel."

The fact was, all these questions swam around in Jessica's head, making her more and more confused as the night went on. They stopped at another church person's house, and the lady who answered the door told them the answer was "the apostle John." Jessica told the others she didn't know very much about him, except that he was one of the twelve opossums, right? Alyssa just stared at her, like she didn't get that Jessica was just kidding.

That was Matt's joke too. Opossums. The problem was, every time she'd asked a Christian something in the past, they always looked like they were reading her some answer off a teleprompter. You know, like TV newspeople read from. And it was always like they got mad at her for asking, like asking was a bad thing. So that's where she was coming from. But she was thinking maybe Matt was going to be different.

"So I have a question for you guys." Jessica felt brave. Or stupid, maybe. She asked herself: *What's the worst thing that can happen, right?*

"What's the story about God creating the world?" She tossed out the question, waiting to see who would snap it up. "Did it really take six days, or longer? I've heard it both ways."

Here's where they come at me with their sound-bite answers, she thought, *and I'm going to go to hell if I don't agree with everything they say, down to the last detail that's maybe in the Bible, or maybe it's not.*

"That's a good question," answered Matt. He looked in the little rearview mirror back at Jessica, while Sarah was gag–ging, probably because she couldn't believe he was saying that to her. "I don't know."

Wait a minute. That wasn't an answer, was it? This was the pillar of the youth group speaking.

"What do you mean, you don't know?" Jessica asked him. "I thought Christians like you were supposed to have all the answers."

He laughed, like she was telling great jokes, which she knew she was not.

"Christians like me know where to go for the answers," he told her, "and we know what we believe. But even Christians don't always agree on every detail. That's why it's okay to ask questions."

Which sounded pretty good to Jessica. But Sarah and Alyssa rolled their eyes. They obviously disagreed with Matt.

"Matt doesn't mean that it's actually okay," Sarah said, "I mean, to actually question your faith."

"Yes, I do." Wow. He wasn't taking anything from her. "Jesus tells us to ask, search, and knock. But even if we do, we're never going to be able to ask a question so big that God can't answer. Right?"

Okay, so this was getting pretty theological, but Jessica liked what she was hearing. By this time they were pulling up to their last house. Or it would be the last house, if they could just get the right answer from the person living there. So now Jessica was really in the question-asking mode, and Matt jumped out of the bug with his camera rolling. He ran up and pounded on the door, like there was a fire. Jessica wasn't sure about how poor Alyssa and Sarah were doing, since their boat had really been rocked.

"How many books in the Bible?" Jessica asked the young mom who answered the door.

She balanced a little kid on her hip, the way moms do. At first she looked like she wasn't going to be able to answer, but then her face lit up.

"Can I phone a friend?" she asked. And since there wasn't anything in the rules about that, they said sure. A minute later she was talking to somebody on her cell phone.

"Sixty-six!" she yelled. "Sixty-six!"

Judging from Matt's whoop, that was the sixty-six-thou-sand-dollar answer, so the team yelled "Sixty-six!" all the way back to the church. Even Alyssa and Sarah got into it, since they had to be tasting the pizza too.

As they pulled up in Matt's crazy yellow and orange and blue Beetle, Jessica thought, *Maybe asking all those questions wasn't such a bad thing, after all.*

Go Ahead,
Stump Me!

Why is it good to ask questions, especially questions about what you believe or what the Bible teaches? (Notice the question is "Why is it GOOD ...? Not just "Why is it OKAY ...?" There's a big difference!)

_____

_____

_____

_____

_____

_____

What do you learn by asking questions, compared to what you learn when you don't?

_____

_____

_____

_____

What questions do you have about God, or about knowing God better? Can all of your questions be answered?

_____

_____

_____

_____

43

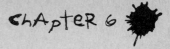

Chapter 6

SOCCER CHAMP

Lissa smiled as her friends Natasha and Sara prayed in the corner of the locker room. This had to be one of the best parts about being on the sixth-grade girls' soccer team!

Natasha prayed for Coach Judy, that she wouldn't lose her temper (Again! Please, Lord!), while Sara prayed that all three of them would be a good witness for Jesus as they played. Well, okay—Natasha and Sara would be playing. Lissa, short for Melissa (and some people said just plain short), would be warming the bench, cheering for everybody else. Oh, and she would be in charge of the first-aid kit. That's what team trainers did.

But that was okay. When it came her turn she prayed for Andrea, of course, only not out loud. Out loud she prayed that they would not get hurt and all that, in Jesus' name, amen.

And there's that moment when everybody looks up and opens their eyes, and it's usually kind of cool. A chance to catch your breath and let the prayer kind of echo around in your head before you run off to something else.

That's when Lissa heard the locker door slam right behind her. She twirled to see Andrea Romaine leaning against her locker, twirling a soccer ball on her middle finger like a cir-cus seal, the way nobody else on the team could do.

And she was watching them.

"I don't know why you bother." Andrea's dark eyes popped a big hole in Lissa's feel-good. "If it's your karma to get hurt, you're going to get hurt. Whether you pray or not."

Karma–shmarma! Lissa would have said something to defend herself and her friends, and she would have explained how they weren't just praying not to get hurt. Really, she would have. But just then Coach Judy's voice rang out through the locker room. And they all knew there was no arguing with the coach.

"Let's go, girls! Hop to it!" Coach Judy could have been a drill sergeant, with a voice that you just couldn't ignore.

"If you get hurt, Andrea," Lissa managed, "it's nothing to do with karma."

But this was the wrong time to talk theology. All they could do was grab their water bottles and sprint out to the field. Good thing they did too, though the last girl out (Sara) got a frosty look from Coach Judy.

"You owe me three extra laps around the field next practice, Miss Pennington."

Coach Judy wasn't kidding. She would collect. But right now they had a game to play, and so they launched into warming up—stretching and sprinting and running pass-and-weave exercises.

"I want to see you MOVE!" Coach Judy even looked like a drill sergeant—as wide as she was tall, with short-short hair tucked underneath a New Jersey Wildcats cap.

But that didn't seem to scare the girls from Oak Grove Intermediate, who were getting ready at the same time on the opposite side of the field. Even from a distance they looked...

"Are those high school girls?" Natasha squinted at their opponents. "Maybe they came to the wrong field."

Sorry, but no. So Lissa didn't stop praying quietly as she watched the game start. For safety. That they wouldn't be killed. And for Andrea, who started against a towering wall of green-and-gold jerseys. In between cheers and peeking through her hands, Lissa added a PS to her prayers.

"And even if we're slaughtered, Lord," she prayed quietly, "help Andrea to see we're your kids."

That didn't seem to stop the Oak Grove girls from walking all over them, though. With cleats. *Bam-bam-bam!* Just like that, Oak Grove was leading, 3 to 0. One of the girls—who seemed to be as tall as a flagpole—sent Natasha flying as they both went for the ball.

"Aw, come on!" Lissa knew a foul when she saw it. But this time the referee didn't seem to notice, and the Oak Grove parents just cheered from the other side of the field, like they were used to winning this way. One Oak Grove mom in particular got right down on the sidelines and yelled at every player by name. Even Coach Judy noticed.

"Wow, she's pretty obnoxious," the coach noted, but under her breath. Lissa wasn't going to agree out loud, but she didn't disagree, either. Meanwhile, the soccer mom kept pacing the field, yelling out advice.

"Watch out for the little dark-haired girl!" yelled the mom.

That would be Andrea, who dived right in after the loose ball, near the goal. Would she have a shot?

"Go for it!" Lissa yelled as loudly as she could, even though the roar of the crowd drowned her out. And Lissa wasn't exactly sure how it happened, but a second later Andrea was rolling around on her back, just in front of the goal.

"Foul!" Lissa thought she'd let the referee know, just in case there had been any doubt. Meanwhile, Coach Judy streaked in to see what had happened. Lissa nearly stepped on her heels.

"You okay?" Coach Judy changed instantly from drill ser-geant to nurse when her girls got hurt. She kneeled on one side of their star forward, Lissa on the other.

"Just—" Andrea looked like a fish out of water, the way her eyes kind of bulged and she couldn't seem to breathe.

"Can you walk?" Lissa blurted out. Andrea looked up at them with tears flooding her eyes. The tough-girl mask had been stripped away. So all Lissa could do was take one of

Andrea's arms over her shoulder, while Coach Judy took the other. And they walked their hobbling star off the field.

"She's okay!" Coach Judy announced to everybody in the stands. "Just got the wind knocked out of her."

It was a little more than that, but the coach's words brought a round of applause as they helped Andrea to the bench and another girl took her place.

"Easy." Lissa figured a cold pack on the ankle would probably help while Andrea got her breath back.

"So much for your prayer, huh?" Andrea mumbled. "I thought God was supposed to take care of our team."

Sure, Andrea meant it as a challenge. Only this time Lissa had a pretty good idea how to answer her.

"You mean, taking care of us like the soccer mom? Yelling at us from the sidelines? That's not what my God is like."

"Hmm."

That was it? No snide comeback. No cutting remark.

Just "hmm."

Well, that was a start. And maybe Andrea didn't get it—yet. But she would. For a moment Andrea's expression softened.

"So then…" Andrea looked down at the team trainer, who was on her knees in front of the bench, holding an ice pack on her ankle. "What *is* he like?"

Lissa smiled. God *had* answered her prayer, after all.

"Thought you'd never ask."

Go AheAD, Stump Me!

Why do you think God doesn't always protect us from danger?

_____
_____
_____

Does it help to pray when you or other people are in danger? Read 1 Peter 5:7 and rethink.

_____
_____
_____

Do you think God will create something good out of something bad that happened? Does Romans 8:28 apply to this question?

_____
_____
_____

Is heaven one of those good things God created?

_____
_____
_____

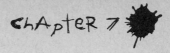

chApteR 7

The GReAt Ticket ScAm

"She's okay." Megan's older brother Andrew pulled her by the sleeve through BJ Lingbloom's front door. "You said you had extras, right?"

BJ frowned but didn't stand in their way.

Well, what did she expect? Her brother and his friends were in ninth grade, after all. But she sure wasn't going to tell anybody she was only in sixth. No way. Maybe she looked older for her age—or she hoped so. She was almost as tall as her brother, anyway.

Still, she couldn't believe Andrew had agreed to let her come along in the first place. Maybe it was her offer to do his dishes for the next two years that sealed the deal. Were they really all going to get free passes to the new amusement park? She couldn't tell just by looking at BJ's face. But now that everybody was there—BJ, Andrew, and four more high school friends that Megan didn't know—it was time to get down to business. Everybody took a seat in the Lingbloom living room. Megan balanced on the arm of a flowered love seat, waiting.

"Okay, everybody." BJ cleared his throat and went on. "So there's good news…and there's bad news."

The other boys groaned, but BJ held up his hands.

"Come on, you guys. First I'll tell you the bad news. The bad news is that my brother isn't coming through with the free passes like he promised."

Louder groans.

"But you said —" Andrew began.

"I know, I know." BJ shook his head. "But he's been acting really goofy lately, ever since the born-again thing. He goes to Bible studies every morning, always talks about Jesus this and Jesus that."

Megan cringed on the inside but tried not to show it. She knew about BJ's brother Tyler. Actually, they'd been praying for him for months.

"Now he says I'm not going to heaven, since I don't believe the way he does." BJ laughed. "Like there's a difference between Buddhists and Muslims and Christians, right?"

Everyone else laughed, even Megan's brother. But if *he* wasn't going to say something, she should. Not that BJ was going to give her a chance, though.

"Yeah, but that's not even the bad part. The bad part is, now he says he can't get any more free passes for us. Says it's stealing. Can you believe it?"

"Bummer." One of the others groaned. Megan thought his name was Brian.

"Yeah," answered BJ, "but I found something in his room that I think you'll like."

He held up the prize with a grin, turning it slowly around so everyone could see the free pass to the amusement park, where BJ's brother worked.

"But that's only one pass." Andrew told them the obvious. "And what'll your brother say if it's missing?"

Megan would have asked the same thing if she'd had enough guts.

BJ dropped his jaw too much, like he was acting.

"You don't actually think I'd *steal* this from my dear old born-again brother, do you?"

Megan gulped again. Had she really begged her brother to let her come?

But BJ wasn't done, and with a smile he picked up a stack of stiff construction paper from the coffee table.

"Hey, I'm not a bad person." The grin never left BJ's face. "All I'm going to do is *borrow* my brother's free pass for a few minutes so we can make our own free passes."

Finally it was sinking in, and by this time Megan's eyes must have given her away. BJ looked straight at her.

"You want to go to the park, right?"

She nodded.

"Okay, so don't worry about it. It's not hurting anybody, and we're not stealing anything. Hey, it's kind of like getting into heaven, right?" He grinned and acted as if he'd just come up with a great new spiritual truth. "Our passes are going to be as good as anybody else's passes. They'll get us in, no problem, Morgan."

"Megan." She couldn't believe she was correcting him, al-most as much as she couldn't believe he was talking to her.

"Megan, right. You know how to use a scanner to make copies?"

Well, she did. And even though the voice in the back of her mind said *no-no-no*, she helped the boys scan the free pass on BJ's flatbed scanner. The paper they used to print ten passes looked and felt almost the same as the real thing. It didn't take long.

"Hey, pretty cool!" Brian held their phony passes up to the light. "Anybody want to try dollar bills? Just kidding!"

Good thing. But Megan tried to keep her hand from shaking as she cut out the counterfeits they'd made. What was she doing?

"Which one's the original?" her brother asked her. She had to search through the pile of paper, though, and even then she still wasn't sure.

"Yeah, it'll work." Once again BJ was in charge as they gathered up the passes and slapped one another on the back. "And Morgan's going to prove it for us."

This time Megan didn't ask too many questions, only closed her eyes and nodded. Too late now, right?

Whether it was or not, an hour later she was moving up in line at the amusement park, clutching her fake pass and sweating. She glanced behind her to make sure Andrew, BJ, and the others were still following, the way they'd planned. If it worked for her, they'd all be in the clear. So she moved ahead, feeling like a fool.

"I'm sorry, Lord," she whispered, her eyes closed, wondering what would happen if she turned and ran. Suddenly she wasn't so sure she wanted to go to this park that much.

"Pardon?"

The ticket–taker looked at her with a puzzled expression, his hand held out.

"Oh, sorry. Nothing." She swallowed hard and gave him the pass, which he tried to scan with a handheld scanner.

But it kept going *boop* and flashing a red light. This was not good.

"That's odd." The ticket guy kept trying as a manager–looking lady came up to help. She tried the scanner, which didn't work for her, either. Megan wanted to scream. Out of the corner of her eye she could see the boys creeping away.

Thanks a lot, guys, she thought.

"Where did you get this?" By this time the manager lady was looking closely at the pass, especially the corner where the ink had smudged from Megan's sweaty hand. To make matters worse, a couple of Megan's friends from school waved at her from the other line.

"See you later, Megan!" said Antonia Parris as she headed for the roller coaster.

At least it looked like Antonia. Megan couldn't tell through her tears. And they were real too, unlike the fake pass. Unlike the older boys who had set her up.

Not that she blamed them, really. Not even her brother, the coward. She'd been the same way. Now she only blamed herself—for letting herself get sucked into this whole ugly mess. And as she walked between a security guard and the manager on their way to the manager's office and more trouble, she could still remember BJ's hollow promise: *Our passes are going to be as good as anybody else's passes. They'll get us in, no problem.*

Only, where was BJ now?

Go Ahead, Stump Me!

Do you think other religions can get you into heaven? Why or why not? What does Jesus say about this in John 14:6?

_____

_____

_____

_____

_____

The way BJ saw it, getting into heaven was sort of like sneaking into an amusement park. Explain what he believed, and why it didn't work.

_____

_____

_____

_____

Why didn't Megan say what she believed when she had a chance? Have you ever felt the same way? What could you do about it in the future?

_____

_____

_____

_____

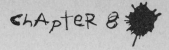

ChapteR 8

PFD MeAns
"PRetty FAt Dummy"

Ah, the smell of the lake at sunset. Ah, the call of the loons. Ah, the...

"We're going in circles again, Franklin."

Gilbert was right. But even though Franklin tried to paddle on the other side, it didn't do any good. Surprise! They were hopeless, all right, and everybody at Silver Lake Camp knew it.

Especially Keith Olderman and Chris Rio, who could have towed a water-skier behind their canoe, if they'd wanted to. As they cruised by, the wave they made behind them seemed like it would tip Gilbert and Franklin's boat over.

"Hey, it's the PFD boys!" Keith shouted across the water at them. By that time, he was so close he didn't need to raise his voice. "We all know what that stands for, right? Although, Franklin, I'm surprised they make a life jacket that actually fits you!"

"Knock it off, Keith." Chris laughed and pretended to scold his friend. He stood up and rode the canoe like a surfer on a board. "They're just doing exactly what their Sunday school teacher told them to. Say your prayers every day and stay out of deep water. Right, Gilly-bert?"

Franklin flinched when an icy spray of cold water hit him square in the face. Keith smacked his paddle again, sending a shower over Franklin and Gilbert. Chris cackled even harder.

"The water's really cold, guys." Gilbert mopped his face with his sleeve. "And you really ought to wear your life jackets. You know the lifeguard would ground you if he saw."

A person would have to know Gilbert to understand that he never said anything mean to irritate anyone. He was just bringing it up because he didn't want Keith and Chris to get hurt or in trouble, period.

"Awww…" This time Chris laid it on extra thick. "The choirboys are a wittle bit gwumpy, and now they're going to tell on us."

Franklin bit his tongue and waited for Gilbert to say something. Instead, Chris slapped the water with his paddle once again, sending a wave that made Gilbert duck and almost tip the canoe.

"Gilbert!" Franklin tried to balance the canoe from the front but only managed to slosh a few gallons over the side. Yeah, it was a good thing they were wearing their PFDs—personal flotation devices. They might be needing them soon.

Keith and Chris wouldn't be coming to the rescue, though. They'd already paddled away and were on their way to harass somebody else. "Time to turn back?" asked Franklin, and Gilbert nodded quietly. It was already getting a little misty on the lake as Keith's laugh echoed across the water.

Only this time they managed to paddle in time with each other, Franklin on one side, Gilbert on the other. Franklin in front, Gilbert in the back. All it took was a little more practice.

"I'm sorry about all that, Gil." Franklin leaned forward as far as he could, though it wasn't quite enough to keep his end of the canoe all the way in the water.

"About what?" Gilbert asked between breaths. As if they both didn't know.

"Oh, come on. The PFD thing. Kids always teasing you about your size."

And it was true. His friend was overweight. But when Franklin looked back over his shoulder, Gilbert only shook his head.

"That's not what bugs me so much," replied Gilbert.

"Then what?"

"It's all the 'choirboy' and 'Sunday school' junk. Just because you and I are the only guys in our cabin who brought our Bibles to camp, we're ... well, you heard it. It gets kinda old."

Sure it did, but Franklin was glad he could hang around with somebody who understood. It helped when the little doubts started to creep into the back of his mind. They talked about their doubts as they paddled on for the next hour. The wind started to whip up little waves, and the sun disappeared behind the woodsy western shore of Silver Lake. They talked about youth group at church, and what they might do or say the next time Keith and Chris got nasty. About girls. About what was for dinner. As they neared the swimming area, Franklin figured the other boys must have slipped in already.

They quickened their stroke when they saw the lifeguard standing on the dock, arms crossed and obviously waiting for them.

"Are we in trouble?" asked Gilbert.

Franklin wasn't sure. They were probably the last ones to return, but the lifeguard didn't even give them a chance to find out.

"You see Keith and Chris?" the lifeguard yelled. "They should have been back an hour ago."

"We saw them go back that way!" Franklin pointed to the far side of the lake, where it widened out and the wind was the strongest. Without even talking about it, they turned the boat around and headed out once more.

"We'll show you!" Gilbert called back.

"My boat motor won't start," replied the lifeguard, "but I've got a call in to the sheriff to see if he can put a boat out there. I'll be right behind you with a light."

Franklin ignored the ache across his shoulders from the past several hours of paddling, digging in and pulling as he never had before. In the growing darkness he could hear Gilbert softly praying. Finally at the darkened west shore, they paused to listen.

"Hear anything?" Franklin thought the loudest thing had to be his heart pounding. But besides the waves slapping their little boat, they heard only wind whistling across the lake and through the pines—and a distant shout?

"That way?" In the darkness Franklin couldn't be sure. Neither could Gilbert. They circled once and made their way toward the middle of Beaver Bay, full speed ahead. Gasping for air, Franklin saw the lifeguard's light flickering behind them, though it was farther away than he'd expected.

They nearly ran over what Franklin thought might be a rock. But than he saw a flicker of moonlight reflected off a pale, scared face looking up at them from the waves. Chris could barely raise his hand above the water, but Franklin grabbed it and held on tight. Keith gripped the side of their boat too, but at least he knew enough not to try to climb aboard and swamp them. Neither was wearing his PFD.

"Our boat tipped," croaked Chris. "But man, am I glad to see you guys, 'cause…"

He couldn't finish; his teeth were chattering too much. But it didn't matter, and Franklin didn't have time to think about how odd those words sounded. Keith and Chris—actually glad to see the choirboys? Well, they could talk later. For now it was enough to thank God, hold on to Chris' cold hands, and wait for the lifeguard's boat to catch up.

Go Ahead, Stump Me!

What would you say to someone who made fun of you for being a Christian? What would you do, if you had a chance? (And don't say, "I'd put ants in their bed"!)

_____
_____
_____
_____
_____

Could cruel comments make you question your faith, the way it did for Franklin in the story? What if it did?

_____
_____
_____
_____

Name three steps you can take to keep your faith strong and healthy. (Hint: What did Franklin and Gilbert do that set them apart? How did they react to Chris and Keith, and what did they do for them?)

_____
_____
_____
_____
_____

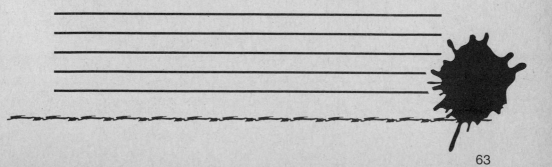

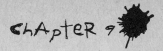

CHAPTER 9

HAPPY FOURTHDAY TO YOU

Brandon chuckled as he stuffed another "China Dragon" firecracker into the can. Safe and sane fireworks? These church kids needed somebody to show them how to have a little fun. So while nobody was looking he'd just surprise them with the Brandon Rogers Special!

"Surprise!" Everyone at the picnic cheered when Shawn's mother brought out the cake— red, white, and blue, with twelve candles shaped like firecrackers. Shawn didn't mind that he was born on the Fourth of July. The good part was that the whole family usually showed up for the traditional party at Hoover Lake Park. People from church sometimes came. Plus, he could invite whatever friends he wanted.

"Be sure to let your friend have a big piece." Mom was always thinking of the guests. And Brandon, the new kid at St. Michael's Christian School, didn't seem to mind—even though he'd already eaten four hot dogs and half a water-melon all by himself. He was a bottomless pit.

"So, Brandon," Shawn's mother asked as she cut more cake, "how did you like St. Michael's? I know you were only there for the last two months, but—"

"It was fine," he answered, loading up with another big mouthful of cake. End of discussion. Of course, there were all kinds of kids at Shawn's school. Lots of Christians, and lots of, well…kids like Brandon.

"So when are the fireworks?" he asked between mouthfuls of cake.

"You mean the big bang?" Shawn looked at his watch, glad they were changing the subject, wondering where the other kids had disappeared to. "As soon as it gets dark. Twenty minutes, maybe. Only it's not such a big deal. We just light off some red, white, and blue sparkler things and push them out in a raft. It's pretty cool out there on the water, but I don't really know why we call it the big bang."

"Yeah, well, back home in Houston, we used to have a really awesome neighborhood party on the Fourth. We launched, like, tons of rockets, firecrackers, the works. The big ones were like a hundred dollars a pop."

"My dad would never let us do that." Shawn chuckled and looked at their modest little fireworks stash down by the beach. Dad had always been pretty strict about staying safe, who got to light the sparklers, all that. While they were wait-ing, though, he thought he'd better ask Brandon more about himself. Make him feel comfortable.

"So do you miss your friends from Houston? Your old school, that kind of thing?"

"School? Yeah, right!" Brandon looked around for a second piece of cake. "I only had one good teacher there, that was Mr. Jacobs, my science teacher. He was really cool."

"Yeah?" Shawn waited for his new friend to explain.

"'He was totally into dinosaurs and evolution and all that. He even had this big picture of that Charles Darwin dude up on the wall. But speaking of big bangs, he was into that theory too. We all had to do a report on it."

"Cool! So did we!" Finally something they had in common, maybe. They started down the little grassy hill toward the beach. "We got to write how we think God created the universe in one big explosion, where everything basically started out in one place, and how lots of scientists are starting to see that the creation stuff in the Bible makes a lot of sense, and—"

He stopped, with Brandon laughing so hard. What was so funny?

"It's not you." Brandon wiped his eye with the sleeve of his shirt. "It's just that the only time Mr. Jacobs ever mentioned God was one time when I heard him in the parking lot, after he shut the door on his thumb. He's not like any of our teachers at St. Michael's."

"Maybe not, but…" Shawn tossed another stone. Why not ask? Brandon had left the door open. "But what about you?"

"Me?" Brandon took his time choosing a smooth stone to skip, then wound up and let loose. "If I told you, you'd kick me out of your Christian birthday party."

"Oh, come on. Really."

Another pause, another stone skipped out across the lake.

"All right, well…I think the big bang idea is cool and everything. Whatever works for you. But I think Mr. Jacobs might have been right. I just don't think God made it happen."

"Huh?" Shawn didn't get it. "Then who did?"

"Nobody."

"You're kidding."

Brandon shook his head. Wow. Shawn might have guessed that's what Brandon thought, but it was still weird to have someone come right out and say so.

"I mean, no offense or anything, but…" Brandon turned back toward the food table, and again the conversation was over. Well, okay. By then it was time to get the big bang going anyway, if Shawn could find his dad. So he ran up to the horseshoe pits and over to the swing sets, but it was getting too dark to tell. Finally he decided his dad might have already headed down to the beach, so a few minutes later he hurried down the path and through the bushes.

"Shawn, wait! Don't go out—"

Shawn heard the voice behind him just as he stepped out onto the gravel beach, just as the flash of light blinded him.

And then he remembered falling over backward, and nothing more until he woke up on the grass, surrounded by people.

"He's waking up," said Shawn's dad. Oh, so there he was. "Everybody, give him some breathing room."

What he really needed was an aspirin.

"Whoa, my head." He felt his forehead, where someone had stuck a large bandage. His temples throbbed. "What…was I struck by lightning?"

Not likely, but that's what it felt like. Some birthday!

"It's all my fault." Brandon knelt next to him, and it sounded like he was crying. "I tried to stop you from going down there after I lit the fuse, but…"

Shawn wasn't quite sure what he'd just heard.

"You lit a fuse? What fuse?"

"I put some firecrackers in a can, and I think a piece of metal might have hit you in the forehead. It was really stupid of me. But I didn't think…"

"It's okay." Shawn was glad he was still in one piece.

But that didn't stop Brandon from saying he was sorry, again and again, in the car and all the way to the emergency room for stitches.

"Really, it's okay." Shawn finally held up his hand as they were sitting in the emergency waiting room, hanging around until Shawn's name was called. Brandon let out his breath, like he'd been holding it the whole time.

"That was sure our big bang, though, huh?"

"Yeah." Shawn did his best to smile. "Only I guess this one didn't just happen by itself, either."

Well, maybe Brandon didn't see it Shawn's way—yet. And Shawn could think of much less painful ways to prove his point about big bangs.

GO AHEAD, STUMP ME!

Can you think of anything that begins to exist without a cause behind it? What are the possible causes of the universe?

_____
_____
_____

Read Genesis 1. Do you think it makes sense that God was behind the starting of the universe? Why or why not?

_____
_____
_____

What would you say to someone who believes that nothing caused the Big Bang?

_____
_____
_____

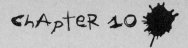

CHAPTER 10

TAKE ME OUT TO THE DERBY

BAM!

Izzy winced and plugged her ears as the big blue car streaked out of nowhere and smacked into the passenger side of the old white station wagon. She peeked over at her older cousin Alex, who was grinning at her.

"What's the matter, Izzy?" He poked her with his elbow. "Don't ya'll have demolition derbies back home in Chicago?"

"Yeah, we do." She had to shout above the roar of the crowd and the crash-roar of the derby. "We call them *rush hour.*"

Well, that got a laugh. But it didn't get Izzy out of the mess she was in: having to sit through the loudest grandstand show in history with her older cousin, her parents, Aunt Nancy, and Uncle John. Watching twenty-five clunker cars in the middle of a dirt football field, crashing into one another until just one was left running. She checked her watch again.

Smash! Another hit. Another cheer. Well, obviously people liked this kind of thing, so Izzy didn't want to be rude. She saw this part of her family only once every summer, when she and her parents visited Atlanta. And she had promised to be sociable. Coming along to the demolition derby was sociable.

She'd also promised to keep praying for Alex and his family. Be a witness.

"If we're not," her mom had asked her weeks ago, "who will be?"

Right. But that was before her cousin had come back home from college with all the answers. Like how obvious it was that humans evolved from monkeys.

Huh? Half the time Izzy had no idea what he was talking about—except that it didn't sound at all like what she'd read in her Bible. Still, she felt like she had to be polite and nod, even when Alex kept showing off all his crazy new ideas.

CRUNCH!

Izzy jumped off the bench, which made Alex laugh all over again.

"Chill out." He pointed at a cloud of smoke. "Look, it's over, see? Number fifty-seven won."

Terrific. The driver of a purple-and-gray wreck waved at the cheering crowd as he circled the other dead and crunched cars.

"Survival of the fittest, huh?" Alex put on that smirk that signaled he was about to pass out a little more college wisdom. "Just one more example of how evolution works."

"You're kidding, right?" This was too lame. He actually believed that smashed cars at the demolition derby proved… what?

"No, look." Alex pointed to a big green car with the back end curled up. "See that Chevy there?"

The one with all the smoke coming out of it?

He went on. "That's a '79. You can tell by the front end."

What was left of it. But Professor Alex wasn't done.

"Then look at that Chevy right next to it. It's a '77, but it came from the same assembly line. The body is almost the same."

"Okay…"

"So that's the example my professor at Tech used to explain it. Cars that look alike. It's how scientists look at fossils too, how they can tell that one life-form comes from the next… You know, evolution."

Oh. By that time they had followed the crowd off the grandstands and were making their way to Uncle John's minivan out in the parking lot. Who was she to argue with a college kid? And yet… something occurred to Izzy about what her cousin was trying to tell her. She turned to him after they'd piled into the backseat.

"Those cars you pointed out…," she started.

"Yup." Alex knew the answers. "Just another illustration of evolution."

"Whatever." This time she couldn't just smile and nod. "I was just wondering, though. Do you think a real person designed the older car?"

"Well, sure." This time Alex's face clouded a bit.

"And did a real person design the newer car too?"

"Sure, but—"

"And would there be a chance the designer might have used some of the same ideas, or maybe some of the same drawings, for both cars?"

Alex frowned and sighed this time.

"That's not the point."

Wasn't it? Izzy tried not to rub it in, just let her cousin stew on it. Yeah, so if the cars looked like they were related, that could mean the same person thought them up. Couldn't it?

Just like in creation. Only in creation it would be the same *God* who used the same kind of plans for the things—and the people—he made.

Good example, Alex, she thought, and she tried to keep from smiling as they drove away from the fairgrounds.

"Thanks for taking us to the derby," she told her uncle John. "Maybe we should do it again next year."

Go AheAD, Stump Me!

What do you think of Alex's argument that cars could help us understand evolution? What's wrong with his argument?

_____
_____
_____
_____
_____

According to the Bible (see John 1:1), who or what made God? When was God created? How is he different from the creatures he created?

_____
_____
_____
_____
_____

How did Izzy use something ordinary like a demolition derby to explain what she believed? What are some ways you can do the same thing?

_____
_____
_____
_____

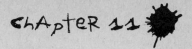

CHAPTER 11

DOUBLE-SPACED

"I'm not saying there couldn't be aliens somewhere." Madison looked out through the windows of their three-seat lunar landing simulator. The earth, which had looked far off before, now nearly filled their view. "I'm just saying I don't *think* so."

"What?" Travis, the flight commander, sat in the middle seat of three. "You don't think out of all those millions and millions of planets out there, life couldn't have evolved on at least one?"

"Who said anything about evolving? I don't—"

"Oh, that's right," he interrupted. "I forgot. You still believe in the Sunday school version."

"If you mean that I believe God created all this…" She meant all the space they could see out their window. The fake stars looked so real. Especially the big blue planet. "Then yeah. A lot of astronauts get up into space and see how God created everything."

The simulator lurched and some lights started flashing. But Travis only chuckled and shook his head.

"Not when they get back down to Earth." He waved his hand at the globe, bigger and closer. They could see the outline of Africa now, and the Atlantic Ocean. "I mean, come on. A little air, a little water, a little heat, a few million years, and there you go. What's so special about this place that it couldn't happen a thousand million times over?"

Madison sighed. Not again. Before they'd come on this field trip to Space Camp, she'd promised herself not to get into any discussions with the class brainiac. As her best friend, Samantha Ortiz, had warned her, nobody out-nerded the Nerd.

"But it's perfect the way it is," she tried. "If the earth were small, we'd hardly have any gravity and so we'd float away."

"Yeah, wouldn't that be cool?" he joked.

"But if the earth were big," Madison explained, "we'd have too much gravity and we'd be like pancakes smashed to the ground. So I don't think it's evolution or chance that gave us a planet that's just the right size. God's fingerprints are all over this."

Travis shrugged the same way he always did when she tried to argue with him, like he didn't want to be confused with the facts. Now an alarm went off as well. Madison pointed at the blinking yellow light.

"Uh…aren't we supposed to be doing something, Travis?" she asked. She was no expert, but it wasn't hard to see.

"Sure. Thrusters off, on my mark. Three-two-one…" Suddenly Travis snapped commands like a shuttle pilot, which only made Madison sweat even more. Uh-oh. She ran her hands across the huge panel of switches and lights in front of her.

"Uh…right," she replied. "Thrusters. Hang on a sec."

Over on Travis' left, Samantha let out a giggle.

"Come on, you two," Travis snapped. "This is why girls don't go to space very much."

"Hey, that's not true!" Madison wasn't going to let that one go. "Lots of women go to space, and they do just as well as the men. Sometimes better."

"Not if they can't find their way around the controls." Travis reached over and flipped a red switch right in front of Madison's face. "There. We just crashed into Siberia because you couldn't find the right switch. Little too much gravity, huh?"

"Leave her alone, Travis." Good for Sam, who finally came to Madison's rescue. "You've been inside this simulator thing a hundred times. This is our first time."

Madison couldn't wait to get out. Her closet back home had more room than the little three-seat fake control cockpit thingie, pretending they were flying to the moon and back.

"All right, you three." The tinny voice of a Space Camp instructor came over the speakers behind their heads. "I think you've done enough damage for one flight."

"Amen." Madison looked up when the overhead hatch opened, and took in a deep breath of fresh air.

"So is that all you can come up with?" Travis challenged her again as he unfolded his skinny frame from the simulator capsule. "A little thing like gravity?"

"You mean, what's so special about the earth?" she asked again to stall for time, while she thought of an answer that would make more sense. "There are lots of other things."

The trouble was, she couldn't quite think of any. By then their Space Camp counselors had already steered the group down the hall to another event, the centrifuge.

"Now we're talking," Travis said a half hour later as they were strapped into a little pod about the size of a sports car.

"It's even smaller inside than the last one." Samantha started breathing kind of funny, and Madison patted her hand so she wouldn't totally freak out.

"We'll look back on this and laugh," Madison whispered to her friend. Right. Saying so might help her believe it herself.

"All right." The staff guy in the navy-blue polo shirt got their attention. "Your pod here is on the end of this thirty-foot arm. We'll shut the hatch over you and start you spinning around, which will make it feel like you're inside a spaceship, taking off."

"C-c-c-ool." Samantha's teeth chattered, and she broke a weak smile.

"How many G's are we going to pull?" asked Travis. The staff guy lifted his eyebrows.

"Sounds like you've done this before."

"Seven times." Travis shrugged. "I did the advanced Space Camp overnighter for my last birthday."

"Good." The staff guy smiled. "Then you can tell your friends there's nothing to worry about. We're only going to try for three G's this time, which is three times the force of gravity you feel when you're standing here on earth. Got it?"

The girls nodded, but Travis only frowned.

"Is that all?" he asked. "Fighter pilots do more than that."

"Well, you're not a fighter pilot." The staff guy smiled as he tightened the spider's web of straps around each of them. "We don't want you blacking out on us."

"Thanks," Madison whispered as the hatch closed. After a couple of seconds and an "all clear" buzzer, they lurched into action. And at first it wasn't so bad.

"Is that it?" Samantha looked over at them with a little smile. Maybe they would survive this, after all.

Or maybe not. Because a moment later Madison felt her head press back into the padded seat. Yikes! Her eyes grew wide, and she could hardly move.

"Feels like…," Samantha began, forcing out the words, "a big hand…pressing my face down."

Madison felt like her cheeks had deflated. Like her eyeballs were going to pop. Like she could hardly look to the side to see if the other two were still alive.

But she did, just in time to see the smile disappear from Travis' face. He gurgled a little, but by this time he looked more like the fish Madison had caught last summer in Lake Peregrine, the way it gasped and its eyes bugged out.

But before Madison could figure out what to do—have mercy!—it was over. Slowly she felt the blood return to her cheeks, and she started to breathe easier. Only things weren't so easy for Travis. Even before they'd stopped all the way, he grabbed for a little paper bag in a rack next to their seats. Like he was going to…

"He's sick!" announced Samantha. Madison didn't know whether to plug her ears or her nose. And she didn't waste any time jumping out of the pod as soon as the doors opened.

"You'll be all right, dude." The staff member helped Travis out last. Everybody who was still in line for the simulator sort of backed up as he walked by, like he had a disease he could give them.

"Ew," said one girl. "What happened to him?"

Madison helped him out of the building into the fresh air. For once he had nothing to say, which really wasn't a bad thing.

"Yeah," she told him. "You'll be okay. You just got a little too much gravity. And gravity's not such a big deal, now, is it?"

Go Ahead, Stump Me!

What would happen to everything in a world without gravity? Would you be able to float around? Would you float out to space? What would happen to all our water?

_____

_____

_____

_____

_____

Why do you think just the right amount of gravity points to a Creator? See Psalm 8:3–4 for a hint.

_____

_____

_____

_____

What would you tell someone who doesn't think there's anything special about our place in the solar system? What if they think it's all chance and the earth just happens to be where it is?

_____

_____

_____

_____

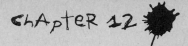

chapter 12

HOLIDAY VS. CHRISTMAS?

"Micromachines? What's that?" Kaela trotted double-time to keep up with Thomas while she checked her watch to see how late they were.

Never mind his micro-whatevers. They had less than five minutes until the biggest band concert of the year, "Christmas by Candlelight." In fact, by now she and Thomas should have been sitting down, tuning their violins. Instead, they were racing down the hall halfway across the school with arm-loads of new music folders.

Yeah, by now everybody and their dog had probably ar-rived, cramming into the bleachers on both sides of the Franklin Middle School gym.

And by now Mr. Morris was probably going ballistic, won-dering what had happened to them. It didn't matter that Kaela hadn't been able to find the right key for the right cabinet to unlock the right drawer containing the folders.

Just hurry.

"It's for Mrs. Snyder's science class," Thomas finally an-swered. Like she should know what that meant.

"I think my little brother used to play with micromachines," she told him. "Those and the little Matchbox cars."

"No, no." He laughed. "Not that kind of micromachine."

So Thomas explained his project as they hustled down the hall. He didn't seem to care that they were in huge trouble.

"And so these micromachines are a part of each cell," he went on, "like a little machine, and they're all working together, see?"

She saw. Maybe she got a C in science last semester, but she didn't think she was *that* dim.

"And there's no way they can all work totally together unless someone designed it that way. Like a factory. Not just chance, but God. Get it?"

She got it. Maybe this wasn't rocket science, after all.

"You mean…" She had a thought. "Sort of like a band?"

Like violins and clarinets, drums and trumpets? All the instruments had to work together, or the song wouldn't click.

Thomas looked over at her like maybe she'd said something smart, for once. The problem was, that meant he wasn't watching where he was going, and he wasn't seeing the classroom door that opened up and smacked him off his feet.

"Thomas, watch—!" Kaela tried to sidestep the pileup, but… never mind. Both their stacks of folders tumbled to the floor in a huge flutter of paper and sheet music.

She groaned and fell to her knees. This was not good. But speaking of Mrs. Snyder, now their science teacher looked as shocked as they probably did. And she was apologizing all over the place.

"I am so sorry, kids!" She tried to pick up a folder or two, but she only mixed things up worse. "I was just grading some papers and remembered it was time for the Winter Concert. Of course I didn't even see you."

She said "Winter Concert," not "Christmas Concert." But this was a public school, after all, and this was the biology teacher at the public school. The woman who believed that we all came from monkeys. But does she possibly believe in God?

"That's okay." Thomas tried to piece together a page one and a page twenty–four, with the right pages in between. The problem was, not all the pages had page numbers. Great, huh?

"We'll get it," Kaela told their teacher. "We're kind of late."

"I'll tell your band teacher it was all my fault." She stuffed another bunch of pages into the folders. Pretty nice of her to act concerned, but that still didn't change how late they were.

"That's it." Thomas was in high gear. He must have finally checked his watch.

Three minutes later Thomas and Kaela finally took their places and quickly tuned their violins while everybody else in the band grabbed their music folders. And when Mrs. Snyder whispered something to Mr. Morris, the air went out of his cheery–red cheeks and he nodded. Maybe running into Mrs. Snyder had turned out to be their Get Out of Jail Free card.

"Hey, what took you guys so long?" asked Andrew Dibble in the clarinet section. "We thought Mr. Morris was going to—"

Mr. Morris didn't give him a chance to finish. With one look he shut down the small talk.

Showtime.

And Kaela knew they needed all the help they could get. Each section needed to play the music a hundred percent. Each *micromachine* had to do their thing just right.

Here goes! She lifted her bow, whispered a little prayer, and launched into their version of Tchaikovsky's "Nutcracker Suite."

It sounded pretty good at first. All their practicing had paid off. Thomas hit a bad note, but nobody noticed.

But then came the page turns. It helps that band music is written so people playing different instruments can turn the page at different times. That way it all blends together.

Not this time. All of a sudden the tuba started playing the bass line from "You're a Mean One, Mr. Grinch." Loud. Then a couple of clarinets started different sections of the "Jingle Bell Medley" and "Santa Claus Is Coming to Town." Huh? The drums added a couple of measures from "The Little Drummer Boy."

Rum-pa-pum-pum.

The whole band melted down in the weirdest jumble of music anyone had ever heard, until Mr. Morris brought it all to a halt with a wild wave of his hands.

And that's when Kaela knew her life was *really* over, except for two things.

One, it wasn't really her fault the pages had gotten mixed up, and that everyone had started playing the wrong notes for a few seconds.

And two, she knew that Thomas now had a really, really good example for his science project. Each instrument was sort of like a micromachine, right? And the music wouldn't sound right unless the conductor kept them on the same page, right? So that's how a real body, made by a Creator, had to work too.

Thomas glanced over at her as if he were reading her mind, and gave her a thumbs–up. Yeah, he was thinking the same thing, all right. Had to be. And if he wasn't, well, she would be sure to tell him.

That is, if they ever survived this concert.

Go Ahead, Stump Me!

Whether in a cell or in a larger machine made by a person, how does a micromachine get started? How does it get put together? How do micromachines figure out how to work together?

_____

_____

_____

What did Kaela finally compare her band to? Why was that a big deal for her to figure out?

_____

_____

_____

The Bible (1 Corinthians 12:12) says Christians are all part of one body. In a way, does that make *us* micromachines?

_____

_____

_____

Have you seen God at work aside from scientific things? Have you ever seen a miracle or something else that can't be explained through science?

_____

_____

_____

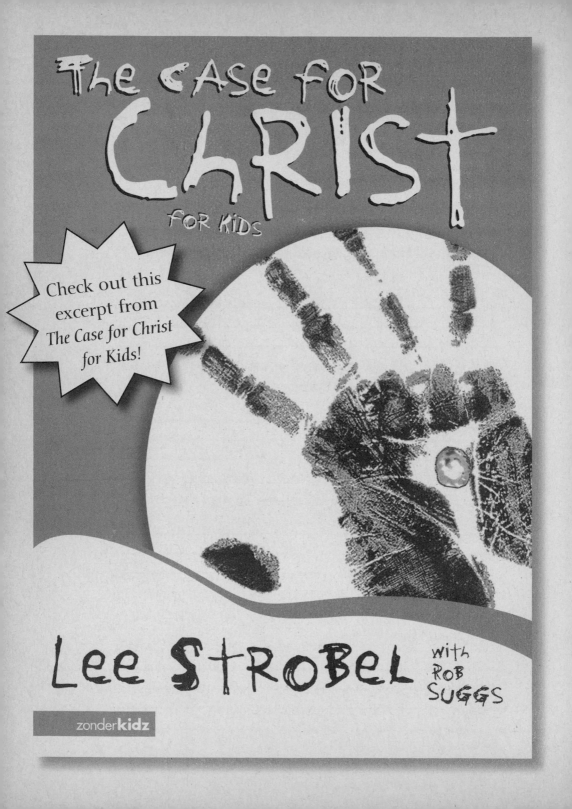

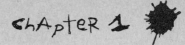

chapter 1

WHO DID THIS GUY THINK HE WAS?

Did you know there is life on the moon?

Hey, what are you laughing at?

Back in 1835, a newspaper called the *New York Sun* printed an entire series of articles that claimed that life had been discovered on the moon. A famous scientist named Sir John Herschel was said to have rigged up a really effective new telescope. He could look through its lens and see exactly what was happening up on the lunar surface. Supposedly he had spotted buffalo, goats, unicorns, and even winged humanoids who built temples!

Also, it seemed as if the moon would make a terrific vacation site. There were beaches, oceans, and forests up there. You could enjoy them as you took a walk in the earthlight.

Some people got pretty excited. But when someone checked with Sir John Herschel, the whole story fell apart. He said he had no new telescope; he had no idea what was on the moon. But he *did* have a good laugh!

This is what we call a "hoax" today—a story created to attract attention. The crazy story made the *Sun* a very popular paper, even after everyone found out the truth.

But it just goes to show you: Don't believe everything you read. When you hear a wild claim, find out the truth for yourself. See if the story holds up.

Actually, that sounds like a pretty good idea for this book. Why not see if the story of Jesus holds up? After all, it's a bigger deal even than goats on the moon. Some people think he was simply a nice guy who taught people to live by the Golden Rule and things like that—just a regular fellow. Others think he never lived at all. Still others believe he was something more than "regular." They say he was the Son of God, and that we should love him and follow him in all that we do.

Golden Rule (gohl-den ROO-el): the virtue of treating others as you would want to be treated.

A lot of differences in those ideas, eh? You need to decide for yourself what you think about Jesus. There are several points for you to look at. First, what did Jesus himself say? Was he crazy or dishonest? And how much evidence is there to support the amazing claims people make about him? Nearly all of Christians' ideas come from the Bible, but how do you know those Bible stories are true? And last there is that matter of coming back from the dead. It's the single most important claim anyone can make about Jesus.

The "Case" Books for Kids

Based on Lee Strobel's Gold Medallion Award–winning *The Case for Christ, The Case for Faith,* and *The Case for a Creator.*

Now those eye-opening bestsellers have been revised by noted children's author Rob Suggs for young people ages eight to twelve—the age when kids begin asking the complicated questions adults themselves struggle to answer. With a companion book—by prolific kids' author Robert Elmer—that gives real-life examples of ways to defend Christianity, these "Case" books are just right for kids who want to stand up for their faith in an unbelieving world.

Written in humorous, light-hearted prose perfect for kids this age, these books analyze the evidence and build compelling cases using historical facts, up-to-date scientific research, and true stories.

- *The Case for Christ for Kids* brings Jesus to life, addressing the miracles, ministry, family, and way of life of Jesus of Nazareth.

- *The Case for Faith for Kids* explains the most abstract articles of faith in ways kids understand.

- *The Case for a Creator for Kids* uses science to strengthen kids' faith, demystifying the creation of the universe with scientific evidence.

- For kids who are sure of their faith but not sure how to defend it, *Off My Case for Kids*—a perfect companion or a stand-alone piece—provides twelve real-life scenarios that empower kids to speak up when challenged.

Each book has plenty of visual interest, using line illustrations, callouts to define terms and phrases, and sidebars to help explain complicated concepts.

THE CASE FOR CHRIST
FOR KIDS

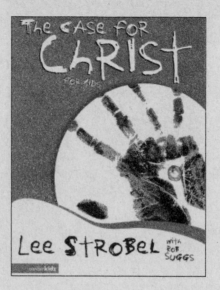

Journalist Lee Strobel analyzed the evidence and built a compelling case for the existence of Jesus. Now his bestselling book has been revised—with kid-friendly terms, humor, and illustrations—to help kids really understand the life and times of Jesus Christ.

SOFTCOVER 0-310-71147-9

Available at your local bookstore!

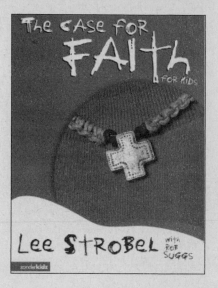